"Love is the way we walk in gratitude."

Joyful greetings of the season from

THE FOUNDATION FOR INNER PEACE

ECHOES
OF
TIMELESSNESS

JOHANNES VAN PRAAG

Published by
Van Praag Publications
P.O. Box 4LA
London W1A 4LA

Graphics by
Julien van der Wal
Geneva

ISBN 0-9515872-0-X   Printed in Switzerland

CONTENTS

"EXEMPLUM DEDI VOBIS"*

Christ gave us an example. He told us "I am the son of God". In fact, I believe the Message was that we all are.
We share the guidance of the Holy Spirit, our Higher Selves, God's presence inside us. This presence is the true"I am" in each of us. The rest is an illusion. This is what makes us "His son".
The Holy Spirit is our participation in reality, and the moments when we do not judge one another or ourselves, the moments when we forgive to a point we see no sin, is when we come closest to true being. Heaven is the total union; the mind becomes entirely the same as this God-part of us, and thus one with all other beings.
These are the principles from which I believe the following pages flowed.
The poems, their content and form, were an irrepressible result of small moments of stillness in a life that had never been quite as hectic, had never allowed for quite so little time to contemplate. It seemed that my active "me" had little to do with their origin; it just embraced the results with happy recognition.

* "I gave you an example", as quoted in the Imitation of Christ by
  Thomas a Kempis

Although this poetry grew from a context of spiritual development that expresses itself in Christian terms, I at least recognise in it some elements of the "Perennial Philosophy" that we all share. I feel for instance that it reflects the basic message of the Bhagavad Gita as much as it does the passages of the New Testament with which I grew up.

The embarrassment that I feel in committing these lines to print sprout of course from the fact that each of those great writings and so many other inspired sources convey the Message so much more importantly. One wonders : "is there a place for these little personal experiences of the Word ?" Here, again, I decided to trust Him who made me write them in the first place and I know that even the smallest contribution that these poems may make was meant to be.

J V P

London, 1990

TRAVELLER

I live the journey once completed

Long forgotten is the path

Yet at this turn I know I am approaching:

Far away I see Your house

CHRISTOPHOROS

Who shall know what burden is heavy

Or why, if it seems to be

Thank you Father for deeming me worthy

For letting me carry Your son

GUIDED

The holy child is still

It knows where I am going

I close my eyes and hold its hand

The sounds of battle fade away

TIME FOR ETERNITY

Your loss in time

is just a dream

You have arrived

and you were never gone

LET ME BE YOURS

Let me be the stone

You drop in the water

Let me be the ripples

ever extending

HOMECOMING

The stones of time ground away

while the gentle eye

looked on and waited

for me to come to my senses

FLOATING FLOWER
for Lai-Ping

From where is your knowledge

How did you know

blown by the wind

both gentle and strong

GRATEFUL

My sail against a grey-black sky

A small white flower on the moss

Your shining hair on your soft skin

You came for me to love

ENCHANTED MOUNTAIN
for Ling-Shan

His hand is in my hand

small and yet firm

I know it stays forever

no matter where he goes

RECOGNITION

I see His face in your face

Son and my Father

I recognise you

you are He

NIGHTMARE

A tear is on his cheek

restless his sleep

Lord, may I always hold him

and breathe Your love into his dream

SHARING

God looks at me through his smile

God speaks to me when he laughs

I see what he sees

And know what he lives

TO A BROTHER

Born into two different worlds

we share this Ray in time

and in our daily doings

I serve my God in you

RENDEZ-VOUS
IN A SMALL CHURCH

I enter Your house

to see Your light

When I go out

it is still warm

and the sun has set

PRESENT-ETERNAL

The time is exactly now

Gone are the past and the future

You have restored my wings

I am forever free

THE PAST UNMASKED

I know it is not here

The world has never been

I am the loved son

I feel the brightness

the distant melody

TEMPTATION

I call upon Your holy name

while sounds of glitter beckon

I call upon my holy name

and know that I have found You

VARIA VITA

I need the waves

I need the wind

I need to swim up-stream

How deep a fall

or rude a shock

before I feel Your hand ?

PRAYER ON A FLIGHT

I see the world I dreamed

all that I thought

ant heap of doing

Let it all be You

Let it be

MISSION

To live this life with open arms

to rise beyond the shadows

I need not ask why I am here

For You will always guide me

THE LAST ILLUSION

Let me forgive the world and its loudness

Let me forgive the good and the bad

Let me see the Rays on the field

and live the Peace above

THE WORD

When all has vanished

differences gone

there is light

and the Word remains